The Essential

Wine Buff

As far as I am concerned there are only two types of wine, those I like and those I don't.

André Launay

The Essential

Wine Buff

Edited by
JENNIFER TAYLOR

ROBERT HALE • LONDON

ISBN 0 7090 5242 1

Robert Hale Limited
Clerkenwell House
Clerkenwell Green
London EC1R 0HT

2 4 6 8 10 9 7 5 3

Printed in Great Britain by
St Edmundsbury Press,
Bury St Edmunds, Suffolk.
Bound by Hunter and Foulis Ltd.

Contents

Contents

Preface

There was a time when the world of wine *seemed* relatively straightforward. I remember my father, in the 1950s and '60s, buying bottles of Châteauneuf-du-Pape, Moulin-à-Vent and Nuits St Georges, which were reasonable in price and reliable. Now these wines are definitely on the pricey shelves, while the really big names such as Chambertin and Romanée-Conti are more expensive still. A Château Mouton-Rothschild 1990 is quoted in a current catalogue at £65; what price a Château Lafite or Margaux decades old?

I think it was André Simon who recounted the following anecdote against himself. He was dining at a wine connoisseur friend's house, and his host would not reveal the identity of the wine at dinner. It was good, even very good, and André Simon expressed his appreciation, but without going over the top. Afterwards, he learnt that it had been an awesomely celebrated vintage of an awesomely celebrated wine. Ah. . . this knowledge would, he admitted, have made him drink it with due reverence. The literature of wine abounds with similar tales.

Now supermarket shelves are crowded out with newer wines – a plethora of names often confusingly similar, with an increasing number of countries contributing to the wine lake (or should that be ocean?). At last year's International Wine Challenge, 6,500 wines from 30 countries were tasted.

Even if wine writers of old did not have the profusion to write about, the wine trade has always been a complex one. Wines from Hungary, Romania and Greece were written about a century ago, while production was increasing fast in Australia and California.

Wine writers were already then complaining that the vocabulary of description was exhausted. Hardly surprising that today's writers have recourse to such strange substances, quite apart from the huge array of fruit and flower comparisons. It seems that wine hardly ever tastes simply of grapes. I have had considerable fun compiling a list of adjectives and phrases used in articles, reviews and books.

There is a very funny moment in the film *Babette's Feast* when a dour Danish Lutheran lady tastes wine for the first time (and a very fine one at that): an expression of disbelief that anything could be so delicious lights up her pinched features, and she makes sure a refill comes her way fast. So, to put us in a convivial mood, first some general quotations about wine and its 'nectareous' qualities.

JENNIFER TAYLOR

That Divine Liquor

Wine drunken with moderation is the joy of the
soul and the heart.

ECCLESIASTICUS, 31:36

. . . that nectareous, delicious, precious, heavenly,
joyful and divine liquor called wine.

RABELAIS
Pantagruel

O thou the drink of gods, and angels!   Wine!

ROBERT HERRICK
Hesperides, 1648

Wine, madame, is God's next best gift to man.

AMBROSE BIERCE
The Devil's Dictionary

9

The love of wine may almost be classed with the innate principles of our very being.

> ANON
> *The Wine-Drinker's Manual,* 1830

By wine we are generous made;
It furnishes fancy with wings;
Without it we should ne'er have had
Philosophers, poets or kings.
> *Wine and Wisdom,* 1710

Is not wine the very essence of laughter?

> MAURICE DES OMBIAUX
> *Le Gotha des vins de France,* 1925

Wine has a drastic, an astringent taste. I cannot help wincing as I drink. Ascent of flowers, radiance and heat, are distilled here to a fiery, yellow liquid. Just behind my shoulder-blades some dry thing, wide-eyed, gently closes, gradually lulls itself to sleep. This is rapture. This is relief.

> VIRGINIA WOOLF
> *The Waves*

Wine is only sweet to happy men.

> JOHN KEATS
> in a letter to Fanny Brawne, 1819

10

Wine, like the rising sun, possession gains,
And drives the mist of dullness from the
brains.
GEORGE CRABBE
The Borough

Wine certainly sets the mind alight and sets the
wits dancing round the central bonfire of genial
emotion. But it is an affair of rosy and capricious
illuminations, a sunset of inspiration, a showery
sunset with a rainbow that soon departs.
SIEGFRIED SASSOON
Diaries, 7 July 1922

Brisk methinks I am, and fine,
When I drink my capering wine;
Then to love do I incline,
When I do drink my wanton wine;
And I wish all maidens mine,
When I drink my sprightly wine;
Well I sup, and well I dine,
When I drink my frolic wine;
But I languish, lower, and pine,
When I want my fragrant wine.

ROBERT HERRICK
Anacreontic Verse

Wine prepares the heart for love, unless you take
too much.

OVID
Remediorum Amoris

Cupid, and *Bacchus,* my Saints are,
May drink, and Love, still reign,
With *Wine,* I wash away my cares,
And then to *Cunt* again.

EARL OF ROCHESTER

A man will be eloquent if you give him good wine.
RALPH WALDO EMERSON
Representative Men

Always hurry the bottle round for five or six
rounds without pressing yourself or permitting
others to propose. A slight fillip of wine inclines
people to be pleased and removes the nervous-
ness which prevents men from speaking –
disposes them in short to be amusing and to be
amused . . .

When you have drunk a few glasses to play the
good fellow and banish modesty if you are
unlucky enough to have such a troublesome
companion, then beware of the cup too much.
Nothing is so ridiculous as a drunken praeses.
SIR WALTER SCOTT
Journal, 22 February 1827
advice on speaking in public at a dinner

Wine vs Water

Dr Johnson recommended to me, as he had often done, to drink water only: 'For (said he,) you are then sure not to get drunk; whereas if you drink wine you are never sure.' I said, drinking wine was a pleasure which I was unwilling to give up. 'Why, Sir, (said he,) there is no doubt that not to drink wine is a great deduction from life; but it may be necessary.' He however owned, that in his opinion a free use of wine did not shorten life.

> JAMES BOSWELL
> *Life of Johnson,* 19 September 1777

Although Water be the most ancient drink, it doth very greatly deject the appetite, destroy the naturall heat, and overthrow the strength of the stomack, and consequently, confounding the concoction, is the cause of crudities, fluctuations, and windinesse in the body.

> DR TOBIAS VENNER
> *Via Recta ad Vitam Longam,* 1637

Though small drink or cold water seeme to quench thirst better than wine because it moystneth and cooleth more, yet wine being more agreeable with nature, and of more subtile substance & operation, is sooner drawne off the members, and consequently sooner satisfies and fils the veines, and so quencheth thirst without any great alteration of the body: whereas water by the great coldnesse thereof, sodainely

14

changeth the body from heat to cold, which is a dangerous thing, as Hippocrates testifieth.

THOMAS COGAN
The Haven of Health, 1636

Because the King had at one time suffered from severe attacks of gout . . . , instead of the champagne he had been used to drinking, they had in more recent times made him drink watered-down Burgundy, so old that it had lost its strength . . . Never did he drink his wine unwatered . . . So much water, so much fruit, unrelieved by any alcohol, lowered his vital spirits and turned his blood gangrenous.

SAINT-SIMON
Letters

It is singular how few healthy tea-totallers are to be met with in our ordinary inhabitants of cities. Glancing back over the many years which this question has been forced upon the author by his professional duties, he may estimate that he has sedulously examined not less than 50,000 to 70,000 persons, including many thousands in perfect health. Wishing, and even expecting to find it otherwise, he is obliged to confess that he has hitherto met with but very few perfectly healthy middle-aged persons successfully pursuing any arduous metropolitan calling under tea-total habits.

DR WILLIAM BRINTON
On Food and its Digestion, 1861

Wine for Health

All the charming and beautiful things, from the Song of Songs to *bouillabaisse,* and from the nine Beethoven symphonies to the Martini cocktail, have been given to humanity by men who, when the hour came, turned from tap water to something with colour to it.

H.L. MENCKEN
Selected Prejudices, Second Series

Sir Joshua said . . . that a moderate glass enlivened the mind, by giving a proper circulation to the blood. 'I am (said he), in very good spirits when I get up in the morning. By dinnertime I am exhausted; wine puts me in the same state as when I got up; and I am sure that moderate drinking makes people talk better.'

JAMES BOSWELL
Life of Johnson, 12 April 1776

Many and singular are the commodities of Wine: for it is of it selfe, the most pleasant liquor of all other, and was made from the beginning to exhilarate the heart of man. It is a great increaser of the vitall spirits, and a wonderfull restorer of all powers and actions of the body: it very greatly helpeth concoction, distribution, and nutrition, mightily strengtheneth the naturall heat, openeth obstructions, discusseth windinesse, taketh away sadnesse, and other hurts of melancholy, induceth boldnesse and pleasant behaviour, sharpneth the wit, abund-

16

antly reviveth feeble spirits, excellently amendeth the coldnesse of old age, and correcteth the tetrick qualities, which that age is subject unto; and to speak all in a word, it maketh a man more couragious and lively both in mind and body.

DR TOBIAS VENNER
Via Recta ad Vitam Longam, 1637

The learned Erasmus, who appears to have been of Anacreon's opinion, that if 'With water you fill up your glass, you will never write anything wise', was extremely fond of Burgundy: a good draught of this generous liquor was, he declared, as new blood in his veins, quickening his pen into brightness and life. He attributed the cure of his gastritis to Beaune wine, and was very desirous to live in that town, *'pour boire'*, as he said, its *'vin sain et délicieux'*.

CHARLES R. WELD
Notes on Burgundy, 1869

There is no doubt that as a remedy Beaune is infinitely more pleasant than bicarbonate of soda, gentian-tonic or even Vichy water.

MAURICE DES OMBIAUX
Le Gotha des Vins de France, 1925

. . . the best utilization of solar energy that we have found . . . Wine really is bottled sunshine.

EMILE PEYNAUD
The Taste of Wine, 1983

Wine, as a restorative, as a means of refreshment when the powers of life are exhausted, as a means of correction and compensation where misproportion occurs in nutrition and the organism is deranged in its operation, and as a means of protection against transient organic disturbances, wine is surpassed by no product of nature or art.

PROF. JUSTUS LIEBIG, *c*. 1832

I have not been very well lately, so I thought I would consult that eminent physician Dr. A. The first thing he said to me was, 'What do you drink?' . . . 'Oh,' I said, 'things in general, anything that's handy.' 'The very worst thing you can do; you should take nothing but a couple of glasses of dry Sherry with your dinner.' I followed his prescription for some time, and getting no better, I resolved to see that distinguished practitioner Dr. B. He immediately asked me what I drank – . . . I said 'only a little dry Sherry.' 'What!' exclaimed Dr B., 'dry Sherry? That accounts for it. You must take nothing but a pint of dry Champagne.' I tried this for a week, and, finding myself still out of sorts, I called upon the distinguished Dr. C. Of course the usual question. And when I replied 'a pint of dry Champagne!' he jumped. 'Poison, my dear Sir, poison! No wonder you're out of sorts. Now, if you take nothing but a pint of Léoville – the very best Léoville mind you – we shall soon put you on your legs again!' I tried this remedy for a fortnight – for I rather liked it – but found no improvement whatever in my health.

So on the recommendation of an old friend, I called on the fashionable Dr. D. The usual question, and then Dr D. exclaimed, 'You should never taste a drop of wine of any description. Take the best Scotch whisky and soda in moderation, and you will be well in a week. I tried this, but became rapidly worse. And then? – *then I consulted myself.* I prescribe for myself. Dry Sherry with soup and fish, a pint of dry Champagne with the rest of my dinner, a pint of Léoville after it, and Scotch whisky and soda with my cigar in the evening. I have tried my own prescription – which combines the wisdom of four distinguished Doctors with my own – for a month, and you will be glad to hear I never felt better in my life.

from PUNCH, 5 February 1887

It is (said the monk) well doctored! Let a hundred devils jump on to my back if there are not more old drunkards around than old doctors!

RABELAIS
Gargantua

When a sensible wine-drinker is confronted by scares and panics concerning the horrors of alcohol he remains unmoved, for he knows very well that his trusty beverage is not mere alcohol, but alcohol modified and corrected by the other and more abundant constituents of wine.

C. E. HAWKER
Chats About Wine, 1907

19

How Much?

'Pray, try it, Sir Austin! Pray, allow me. Such a wine cannot disagree at any hour. Do! I am allowanced two glasses three hours before dinner. Stomachic. I find it agree with me surprisingly: quite a new man.'

GEORGE MEREDITH
The Ordeal of Richard Feverel

'A bottle, madam? A whole bottle? Do you know how large a whole bottle is?'

a British Rail steward to
ELIZABETH DAVID, quoted in
An Omelette and a Glass of Wine

The *City Press* quotes a manuscript on parchment attached to an ancient painting removed in 1803 from the old Bull Inn, Bishopsgate Street:

'Portrait of Mr Van Dorn, a Hamburg merchant. Belonged to a club called "The Amicable Society", held at the Bull Inn, Bishopsgate Street, for a period of 22 years. During the above period he drank 35,680 bottles of wine . . . averaging at nearly four bottles and a half per day; and did not miss drinking the above quantity but two days – the one of which was the burial of his wife, and the other the marriage of his daughter, and lived till he was ninety years of age. Painted by Mr Hymon, in the year 1743.'

CHARLES TOVEY
Wit, Wisdom and Morals Distilled from Bacchus, 1878

Some time ago I read of fourteen octogenarians living in the little commune of St Julien Beychevelle, who, all their lives, had taken their quota of wine (claret), and they joined together to give a celebration of the event, a kind of tribute to Bacchus. Some might regard these as exceptional cases, drinking a bottle of wine daily and living to so great an age. But it is not so. Statistics prove the same in the wine-growing districts of Spain and Portugal, Italy and Greece.

CHARLES WALTER BERRY
A Miscellany of Wine, 1932

Red wine is the most effective drug yet discovered for the prevention of heart disease.

PROF. SERGE RENAUD of the French National Institute for Health, in a 1991 survey

The above survey was investigating why the French have a low incidence of heart disease although they don't deprive themselves of pâtés, sauces and cheeses. Then in May 1995 a Danish survey of 13,000 men and women over twelve years reported its findings that drinking three to five glasses of wine a day protects against heart disease. While previous research assumed that it is alcohol which is protective, the Danish study suggests that it is the antioxidants and flavonoids in red wine, particularly in the skins.

21

The last twenty years of the reign of George II,
and the ten years of his eldest son, were
singularly remarkable for excessive wine
drinking . . . Princes, judges, clergymen, the
noblest of the land, rather prided themselves
than otherwise on such social excesses. To drink
less than two bottles of wine at a dinner table
gave a man the character of a milksop. Your
steady-going guest was content with three
bottles, but if you were a person of mark it was
indispensable that you should empty a fourth
bottle. Bumper glasses were the rule, and you
were expected to fill your glass whenever the
decanter came round. The stronger sort of wines
were almost invariably used . . . Mr Croker in his
Book of Reminiscences, declared that, when a
very young man, being invited to dine with
royalty, and knowing that his stomach would not
bear the enormous consumption of wine, he
provided himself with a large sponge, and
secreting it in his napkin, returned the wine from
his mouth to the sponge, and rid himself of the
accumulation by squeezing it under the table.

CHARLES TOVEY
*Wit, Wisdom and Morals Distilled from
Bacchus*, 1878

The wines were chiefly port, sherry and hock;
claret and even Burgundy being then designated
'poor, thin, washy stuff'. A perpetual thirst
seemed to come over people, both men and
women, as soon as they had tasted their soup; as,
from that moment, everybody was taking wine

with everybody else till the close of the dinner; and such wine as produced that class of cordiality which frequently wanders into stupefaction. How all this sort of eating and drinking ended was obvious, from the prevalence of gout.

CAPTAIN R.H. GRONOW
Reminiscences and Recollections, 1810–1860

There is hardly anything that you can't 'walk off', and we walked off this pleasing but perilous predicament.

GEORGE SAINTSBURY
Notes on a Cellar-Book, 1920

Good Advice

Drinke first a good large draught of Sallet Oyle, for that will floate upon the wine which you shall drinke, and suppresse the spirites from ascending into the braine. Also what quantitie soeuer of newe milke you drinke first you may well drinke thrise as much wine after, without daunger of being drunke. But howe sicke you shall bee with this preuention, I will not heere determine, neither woulde I have set downe this experiment, but openly for the helpe of such modest drinkers as sometimes in companie are drawne, or rather forced to pledge in full bolles such quaffing companions as they would be loth to offend.

SIR HUGH PLAT
The Jewell House of Art and Nature, 1594

The chief thing in the art of drinking wine is to keep within those salutary limits which mark the beneficial from the pernicious. In good society, in the present day, this line is well defined; but . . . the difficulty is to keep the mean in those cases where others have no regard to it. This is best done by studying self-respect, and the art of saying 'no' when the necessity for saying 'no' is strongly felt. The courage to do this, and that absence of all fear of being accounted singular . . . will prevent suffering in stomach or moral character.

> CYRUS REDDING
> *Every Man His Own Butler*, 1839

I drink one glass for health, a second for refreshment, a third for a friend; but he that offers a fourth is an enemy.

> SIR WILLIAM TEMPLE

Towards evening, about supper-time, when the serious studies of the day are over, is the time to take wine.

> CLEMENT OF ALEXANDRIA
> *Paedagogus II*

Love wine like a constant mistress; never abuse it, and you will find it bring no sorrows.

> CYRUS REDDING
> 'Wine Sayings of My Uncle'
> *Every Man His Own Butler*, 1839

As Natural as Bread

It is salutary for an Englishman to live for a while in a wine-growing country . . . where wine is neither a symbol by which snobs can demonstrate their wealth or their taste, nor a means of fuddlement, but as natural and as necessary as bread.

CYRIL RAY
Ray on Wine

If we consult experience, the cheapness of wine seems to be a cause, not of drunkenness, but of sobriety . . . On the Continent, where wine is cheap, as in France, and where the quantity drunk seems to us quite enormous, . . . drunkenness is hardly known.

ADAM SMITH

Marc-Antoine Sand was born this morning . . . He is big and strong and he looked me in the eyes with an attentive and deliberate air when I received him all warm, into my apron . . . He was dipped into a bath of Bordeaux wine in which he kicked about with marked satisfaction. This evening he has taken the breast voraciously.

GEORGE SAND
in a letter to Alexandre Dumas *fils*,
14 July 1863

The vine must have been known in this country
at a very early period, since we find it mentioned
in the writings of Tacitus, who observes, 'In this
island there is no intense cold, and besides the
olive and the vine, and other fruit-trees natural
to warmer climates, the soil produces corn in
considerable quantities.'

  JAMES L. DENMAN
  The Vine and Its Fruit, 1864

This region (Gloucestershire) is more thickly
planted with vines than any other part of
England, and they have more plentiful crops with
a more delicious taste. For the wine does not
cause the mouths of its drinkers to twist ruefully
at its bitterness, and indeed yields nothing to
French wines in sweetness.

  WILLIAM OF MALMESBURY
  De Pontificum Anglorum, 1125

An English autumn, though it hath no vines
Blushing with Baccant coronals along
The paths, o'er which the far festoon entwines
The red grape in the sunny lands of song,
Hath yet a purchased choice of choicest wines;
The claret light and the Madeira strong.
If Britain mourn her bleakness, we can tell
 her,
The very best of vineyards is the cellar.

  LORD BYRON
  Don Juan

In the Cellar

A cellar without wine, a home without woman, and a purse without money, are the three deadly plagues.

> CYRUS REDDING
> 'Wine Sayings of My Uncle'
> *Every Man His Own Butler*, 1839

The cellars of Scaurus were renowned, as he had been able to collect three hundred thousand amphoras of almost every kind of wine known – as many as 195 different varieties . . . Scaurus took greater care of his cellars than of his reputation, since he consorted with the most corrupt men in Rome; but he would not tolerate that anything that might corrupt his wine should come near his cellar walls. He once nearly divorced his wife because she had visited the place at a time when she was indisposed in the way that women are; which could, according to him, make his precious wines turn sour.

> ALEXANDRE DUMAS
> *Le Grand Dictionnaire de cuisine*, 1873

Choose your cellar, whenever it is possible, in the live rock beneath or close to your house, where the situation will admit of it; this, however, is not frequently the case . . . .

The majority of wine-cellars in private houses in large cities are not at all adapted for expensive delicate wines . . . Foul air is frequent in them, arising from fissures between the joints in the brickwork; the carriages above shake the street under which they are too often built, and communicate the tremor to the wine . . . The ascent and mingling of the particles deposited by the wine, from the rumbling of carriages, will also be caused, in shallow cellars, by thunder or the firing of artillery.

> CYRUS REDDING
> *Every Man His Own Butler*, 1839

The wine cellar must be of a temperate heat, between 50°and 60° Fahrenheit; and should it be necessary to employ more than one place for storage, the coldest should be selected for sparkling wines, the next for the wines off France, Germany, Italy &c, and the warmest for port, sherry, and other similar descriptions.

> EDWARD L. BECKWITH
> *Practical Notes on Wine*, 1868

Frequently the space under a staircase is thought good enough for the purpose, but even this is better than being next the kitchen fire or laundry flues. Others, again, are in some back or front area, enjoying a temperature of zero in winter, and 60° or 70° in summer.

THOMAS GEORGE SHAW
Wine, the Vine, and the Cellar, 1863

Provided you avoid not much more than a ten-degree difference between winter and summer temperatures, you can cellar wines up to 70°F, and as low as 45°F. At the upper end of the scale, all that happens is that your wines will mature more quickly.

JANE MacQUITTY
writing in *The Times*, May 1993

All wines have not the same time of continuance; for there are some, which by reason of the weaknesse of their heat, cannot long be kept, as White-wine, and Rhenish-wine; for these, and such like, doe in six or seven months, or within, according to the smalnesse of them, attaine unto the height of their goodnesse, and after a yeere, doe begin to decline, and lose much of their goodnesse, especially the smaller sort of them. But the stronger sorts of wines, as Sack, Muskadell, Malmsey, &c. are best, when they are two or three years old: for these . . . doe a long time reserve their perfect vigour.

DR TOBIAS VENNER
Via Recta ad Vitam Longam, 1637

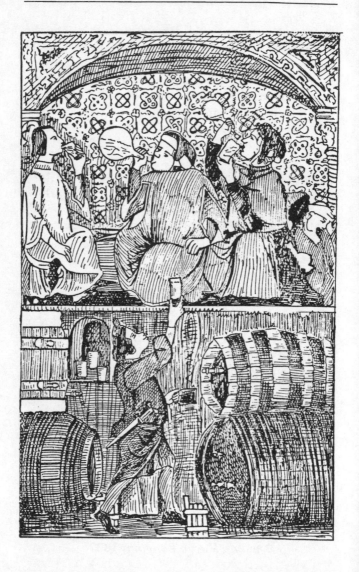

The great glory of Voisin's is its cellar of red wines, its Burgundies and Bordeaux. The Bordeaux are arranged in their proper precedence, the wines from the great vineyards first, and the rest in their correct order down to mere bourgeois tipple. Against each brand is the price of the vintage of all the years within a drinkable period, and the man who knew the wine-list of Voisin's thoroughly would be the greatest authority in the world on claret.

LT.-COL. NATHANIEL NEWNHAM-DAVIS
The Gourmet's Guide to Europe, 1908

It is almost a loss of time to go into a cellar without making memoranda of every cask and bottle tasted, and I therefore made a point of invariably doing this, to gain knowledge, and for future reference. The following (without the prices) is a literal extract from my Note-book: . . .

No. 716 La Tache, 1858, superb for flavour
   715 Grande Rue, 1858, same price as La Tache, but still finer
   717 Romanée-Conti, 1858, 14 l. dearer than the above, finest wine ever I tasted
   660 Chambertin, 1858, very high peculiar flavour, but not very agreeable.
   548 Richebourg, 1857, 6 l. cheaper than the 1858, not so good.
   545 La Tache, 1857; I prefer the 1858.
   541 Chambertin, 1857, extraordinarily delicate, and fine flavour.

THOMAS GEORGE SHAW
Wine, the Vine, and the Cellar, 1863

My Scotch terrier . . . followed me one day without my knowledge, saw a rat, dashed at the bin, and I immediately found him yelling with fear and struggling with the débris and froth of two magnums of champagne. If he had got the rat it would have been some consolation for a rather expensive kind of sport.

GEORGE SAINTSBURY
Notes on Cellar-Book, 1920

Take care of good wine and good wine will take care of you.

CHARLES WALTER BERRY
A Miscellany of Wine, 1932

Wine and Food

Dogges of nature doe abhorre wine. Whereof hath growne that Latine proverb *Caninum prandium*, a dogs dinner, where is no wine at dinner or supper.

THOMAS COGAN
The Haven of Health, 1636

Wine . . . the intellectual part of the meal.

ALEXANDRE DUMAS
Le Grand Dictionnaire de cuisine, 1873

decanter, n. A vessel whose functions are most envied by the human stomach.

AMBROSE BIERCE
The Enlarged Devil's Dictionary

The stomach is the real test-tube for wine.

DR ROBERT DRUITT
Report on Cheap Wines, Their Use in Diet and Medicine, 1873

As a wine drinker but not a wine expert one's tastes are constantly changing.

ELIZABETH DAVID
An Omelette and a Glass of Wine

Drawing a cork is like attendance at a concert or at a play that one knows well, when there is all the uncertainty of no two performances ever being quite the same.

GERALD ASHER

The art in using wine is to produce the greatest possible quantity of present gladness, without any future depression. To this end, a certain degree of simplicity is essential, with due attention to seasons and kinds of food, and particularly to the rate of filling the glass. Too many sorts of wine confuse the palate and derange digestion.

THOMAS WALKER
The Art of Dining, 1881

A man's palate can become saturated, and after three glasses the best of wines produces only a dull impression.

BRILLAT-SAVARIN
La Physiologie du goût

To say that with soup one has to serve a Montrachet or a white Hermitage, with fish a Chablis, Pouilly or Graves, with the roast a Saint-Julien or Pommard, with game a Château Laffitte or Chambertin, is certainly very judicious, but it is inadvisable to make rules on the subject. While it goes without saying that a heavier wine should be drunk with a strong-flavoured dish, the only gradation to follow in the order of wines is from the good to the better, for it is realities, not etiquette, that count . . . All the rest is literature.

MAURICE DES OMBIAUX
Le Gotha des vins de France , 1925

Do not force your opinion of a wine down the throats of your guests. Patiently listen to theirs. You will have lots of fun.

> CHARLES WALTER BERRY
> *A Miscellany of Wine*, 1932

Never press wine on a guest; it is ill-mannered.

> CYRUS REDDING
> 'Wine Sayings of My Uncle'
> *Every Man His Own Butler*, 1839

This wine should be eaten, it is too good to be drunk.

> JONATHAN SWIFT
> *Polite Conversation*

Legendary Vintages

The best wine . . . that goeth down sweetly, causing the lips of those that are asleep to speak.
SONG OF SOLOMON, 7:9

Excellent wine generates enthusiasm. And whatever you do with enthusiasm is generally successful.
PHILIPPE DE ROTHSCHILD

. . . the connoisseur's intellectual ecstasies over a great wine.
H. WARNER ALLEN
Through the Wine Glass, 1954

He fetch'd me gifts of varied excellence;
Seven talents of fine gold; a book all framed
Of massy silver; but his gift most prised
Was twelve great vessels, fill'd with such
rich wine
As was incorruptible and divine.
HOMER
The Odyssey, George Chapman's translation

Wines that, heaven knows when,
Had suck'd the fire of some forgotten sun,
And kept it through a hundred years of gloom.
ALFRED, LORD TENNYSON
'The Lover's Tale'

Then wine bottles were brought up, carefully sealed and labelled. 'FALERNIAN, CONSUL OPIMIUS, ONE HUNDRED YEARS OLD.' While we were examining the labels, Trimalchio clapped his hands. 'Wine has a longer life than us poor mortals,' he sighed; 'so let us refresh our palates. Wine is life. I am giving you real Opimian.'

> PETRONIUS
> *The Satyricon*

'May this cup be my last, but it is the best wine I have drunk at Pompeii.'

'Bring hither the amphora,' said Glaucus, 'and read its date and its character.'

The slave hastened to inform the party that the scroll fastened to the cork betokened its birth from Chios, and its age a ripe fifty years.

'How deliciously the snow has cooled it,' said Pausa.

'It is just enough.'

'It is like the experience of a man who has cooled his pleasures sufficiently to give them a double zest,' exclaimed Sallust.

'It is like a woman's No,' added Glaucus, 'it cools, but to inflame the more.'

> LORD LYTTON
> *The Last Days of Pompeii*

Lord Harrowby mentioned a curious circumstance respecting the age of wine. He told us he had in his cellar in London some bottles of wine considerably more than one hundred years old. They had been in possession of him and his father for very many years. The bottles were marked 1680. He had never tasted the liquor but once, and that was when the foreign ambassadors dined with him a few years ago. He described the liquor as perfectly sound, a white wine, but unlike any wine he had ever tasted. Lord Harrowby said he believed it was the oldest wine in the world. Very possibly, I should think.

WILLIAM DYOTT
Diary, 5 January 1829

There is no money, among that which I have spent since I began to earn my living, of the expenditure of which I am less ashamed, or which gave me better value in return, than the price of the liquids chronicled in this booklet.

GEORGE SAINTSBURY
Notes on a Cellar-Book, 1920

We are now to have a Magnum of 1868, Romanée ... My word! there's a wine ... What did you say?
'I was making a suggestion that we might all stand in silence for half a minute, glass in hand, to offer heartfelt thanks to the Giver of such good things.'

CHARLES WALTER BERRY
Viniana

Until one can convince the world that Romanée-Conti is a wine rather than an investment bond, the future is very bleak.

AUBERON WAUGH
'Burgundy Now and Then'

In truth it was the strangest bottle of wine I have ever drunk . . . The former great taste was still in there somewhere; one moment it was on your tongue, the next it was gone.

ROBERT DALEY describing an 1806 Lafite
Portraits of France, 1991

It tasted like it still had a wine taste, but not very good.

WILLIAM SOKOLIN, New York wine dealer, on a 1787 Château Margaux from the cellar of Thomas Jefferson, for which he had paid £287,000, in 1994

Vin de Table

I never quite got over a scientific lecturer, who contended that the chemical analysis of Château Lafite and that of some Hungarian *ordinaire* being quite the same . . ., it was absurd to give five pounds a dozen for the one when you could get the other for twenty shillings.

GEORGE SAINTSBURY
Notes on a Cellar-Book, 1920

The great point about really fine wines is that one cannot drink them with any pleasure by one's self.

GEORGE RAINBIRD

Pliny used to drink Falernian wine, which was expensive. He would sometimes invite to his table a number of newly freed slaves, and an acquaintance of his . . . commented that on those days the Falernian wine must go down very quickly indeed. 'Forgive me', said Pliny, 'when my freed men dine with me, they do not drink my wine; I drink theirs.'

ALEXANDRE DUMAS
Le Grand Dictionnaire de cuisine, 1873

Last week, I had to offer my publisher a bottle that was far too good for him, simply because there was nothing between the insulting and the superlative.

A.J. LIEBLING
Between Meals

Never drink bad wine out of compliment; self-preservation is the first law.

> CHARLES TOVEY
> *Wit, Wisdom and Morals Distilled from Bacchus*, 1878

Let us give wine – its selection, care, and tasting – all the attention it deserves, but we should not become like certain gastronomes who make a mystery of it, only accessible to the initiated.

> PIERRE ANDRIEU
> *Les Vins de France*, 1939

The gastronome is less concerned with the vintage than with knowing if the wine is ready for drinking. It does not mean that one does not like to know the provenance and status of the wine, but the host who thinks it amusing to make his guests guess name and year is childish.

> MAURICE DES OMBIAUX
> *Le Gotha des vins de France*, 1925

Never guess at a vintage. Acknowledge you do not know, which is more often than not correct.

> CHARLES WALTER BERRY
> *A Miscellany of Wine*, 1932

Can name his claret – if he sees the cork.

> O. W. HOLMES
> *The Banker's Secret*

It is difficult to enjoy a good wine in a bad glass.
EVELYN WAUGH
Wine in Peace and War

The wines that one remembers best are not necessarily the finest that one has tasted, and the highest quality may fail to delight so much as some far more humble beverage drunk in more favourable surroundings.
H. WARNER ALLEN
A Contemplation of Wine, 1950

If in a restaurant you have an expensive wine you do not tip ten per cent on that, nor, in restaurants where ten per cent is charged for the service, has the proprietor a right to ten per cent on his wine. The theory of the tip or the ten per cent is that they are gauged on the amount of service the attendant puts in. As it gives no more trouble to bring a hundred franc bottle of wine to the table than one costing five or fifteen francs it would be absurd to give the waiter who brings it ten francs. But of course if the wine calls for special care in carrying from the cellar, basketing, *chambrer*-ing, uncorking and pouring, you give the *sommelier* a tip all for himself – supposing the results to be satisfactory. But watch his every movement, test the heat of the wine against your cheek and inspect your cork with minute attention so as to be sure that it is newly drawn.
FORD MADOX FORD
Provence

Never say the number, because it suggests that you are unable to pronounce the name of the wine you are ordering.

STEPHEN POTTER
One-upmanship

Wine Writing

Chose your wyne after this sorte; it must be fyne, fayre, and clene to the eye; it must be fragraunt and redolent, havynge a good odour and flavour in the nose; it must sprynckle in the cup when it is drawne . . .; it must be colde and pleasaunt in the mouthe; and it must be strong and subtyll of substaunce.

ANDREW BOORDE
The Breviarie of Health, 1598

Before even it has reached the soft palate, so soon as it is felt by the sense of touch upon the lips, there seems an electric telegram diffused over the remotest twig of every nerve.

DR ROBERT DRUITT
Report on Cheap Wines, Their Use in Diet and Medicine, 1873

If, when tasting wine, you close your eyes and flowers appear before your inner eye then the wine has bouquet – the greater the wine the more concentrated its bouquet.

LOUIS VAUDABLE, owner of Maxim's
writing in *Life,* January 1966

The bouquet of wine comes like a sunbeam, and must be enjoyed at the moment.

CYRUS REDDING
'Wine Sayings of My Uncle'
Every Man His Own Butler, 1839

There can be no vocabulary of tasting unless wines have many complex qualities which are worthy of comment . . . There are millions of bottles of neutral, flabby and impersonal wines about which the taster can say nothing once he has spat them out.

> EMILE PEYNAUD
> *The Taste of Wine*, 1983

. . . describe the indescribable.

> EMILE PEYNAUD
> *The Taste of Wine*, 1983

. . . elegant verbal juggling over a glass.

> P. POUPON
> *Pensées d'un dégustateur*, 1975

There is more rubbish talked about wine and wine tasting than anything else. It is the perfect subject for the snob, the one-up man, the bore.

> ANDRÉ LAUNAY
> *Caviare and After*

We cannot at present coin new words to express sensations; thus it is that we are forced to call some wine *grapy,* and to compare others to a wine already known, such as Madeira.

Wine being grape-juice fermented, should taste of grapes. Some wine has clearly come from grapes greenish, and not over-ripe, as Moselle and Rhine wines . . . Some wine tastes of grapes fully ripe, mature, yet not luscious; some of grapes dead ripe and luscious, as Tokay and Château Yquem; many of grapes with musky perfume, as Muscat, &c; some of grapes dried, as Cyprus and Visanto; some of grape-juice concentrated by boiling, as Como, brown Sherry, Tent, &c; some of withered grapes, as certain Sherries; some of no grapes at all.

> DR ROBERT DRUITT
> *Report on Cheap Wines, Their Use in Diet and Medicine,* 1873

And the wine tastes of grapes – unusual, this: most wine tastes grassy or hyacinthy or beechy or plasticiney or nasturtiumy or gitaney or moron-on-food-and-drink-showy.

> JONATHAN MEADES
> writing in *The Times,* 11 June 1994

. . . the agonising and often excruciating acrobatics off those whose duty it is to enlighten the baffled consumer.

> RONALD SEARLE
> *The Illustrated Winespeak,* 1983

Words of Praise (mostly)

Big	plump
rugged	round
muscular	voluptuous
masculine	bosomy
burly	full figure
chunky	seductive
punchy	gorgeous
hefty	succulent
brawny	fleshy
robust	opulent
gutsy	overblown
aggressive	spanking
bouncy	vivacious
bumptious	flirty
exuberant	luscious
friendly	lush
cheerful	silky
racy	angular
vibrant	lean
vigorous	spindly

insolent
lowering
brooding
majestic
classy
aristocratic
decadent
sophisticated
elegant
steely
lots of backbone
flabby
tooth-gripping
searingly acidic
tangy
savoury
spritzy
pungent
chewy
gulpable
moreish

gawky
skinny
stringy
austere
restrained
reticent
discreet
dumb
pithy
mellow
plummy
dusky
inky
cloying
rustic barnyard
earthy
sweaty
musky
murky
zingy
zippy

a cracker, a firecracker, a humdinger
a love-it-or-loathe-it-but-never-fail-to-
recognize-it kind of wine
red gut rot; blood-guts-and-thunder
a real mouthfiller; blockbuster fruit
a dinosaur of a red
mindnumbingly intense
sheer tooth-rattling-delight
an iron fist in a velvet glove
'winy'

If so many fruit associations are
found in wine by wine writers,
the answer is, according to
recent research at the Univer-
sity of California and elsewhere, that the same chemical
compounds are found in fruit and
wine. So if you think that beaujolais smells of
bananas the reason is the presence of amyl acetate
in the gamay grape. Here then are some of the
flavours detected by current writers.

The Fruit Bowl:
Citrus, lemon, orange, grapefruit
berry, blackberry, blackcurrant, raspberry, wild
   strawberry, mulberry, redcurrant, loganberry,
   blueberry, bramble, gooseberry
cherry, apricot, peach, damson, pear, apple,
   greengage, rhubarb
banana, pineapple, melon, mango, lychee,
   coconut, prunes, raisins

The Vegetable Patch:
Asparagus, celery, beetroot, cabbage, green
beans, green peppers, mushrooms, truffles

The Herb Garden:
Angelica, aniseed, basil, lavender, thyme, mint,
oregano, rosemary

The Spice Box:
Green peppercorns, black pepper, vanilla, clove,
cinnamon, ginger

The Garden Border:
roses, violets, gardenia petal, sweet peas,
    honeysuckle
hawthorn blossom, elderflowers
eucalyptus, gumtree leaf
sandalwood
nettles
meadow grass
straw

Foodstuffs:
hazelnuts, walnuts, chestnuts, almonds,
    pulverized nuts
brioche, yeast, fresh bread, toast
honey, caramel, strawberry jam, boiled sweets,
    creamy toffee, barley sugar, orange
    marmalade, butterscotch, marshmallow,
    marzipan, lemon curd, glacé fruit, liquorice,
    sherbet, crème brûlée
biscuits, Christmas pudding, fruitcake
lemon cheese, cheese rind
meat, smoky bacon, game
tobacco, tea-leaf, jasmine tea, lapsang souchong
coffee

Miscellaneous:

Oil of Ulay	paint thinner
glycerine	linoleum
pencil shavings	dirty old socks

Nice combinations:
chocolate and leather
petrol and lemon sherbet
dirty, mousy, wet dog
wet dog and old cologne
strawberry jam, compost and cabbage
damson fruit, kid glove leather and fish oil
the whole of the Bodyshop in a glass
cut grass, gooseberries and a little whiff of tomcat
cat's pee on a gooseberry bush

The Land of Claret

France is the vineyard of the earth. Her fertile soil, gentle acclivities, clear sunny skies, and fine summer temperature, place her, in conjunction with her experience and the advantages of science applied to vinification, the foremost in the art of making the juice which so gladdens the human heart.

CYRUS REDDING
A History and Description of Modern Wines, 1833

Our sail up the river was delightful . . . The country adjacent is sandy, but is famous for producing the Medoc & other wines that are counted the best in France.

The Hills and vales were covered with Vineyards of a rich & lively green to which the white walls of the Villages and Chatteaux afforded a pleasing contrast.

WASHINGTON IRVING
Journal of a Tour through France and Italy, 1 July 1804

The country all about it is covered with precious vineyards, sources of fortune to their owners and of satisfaction to distant consumers; and as you look over to the hills beyond the Garonne you see them in the autumn sunshine, fretted with the rusty richness of this or that immortal *clos*.

HENRY JAMES in Bordeaux
A Little Tour in France, 1884

53

If Mr Norris's Gascon wine prove not excellent good I am shamed for ever, for I made thereof no small boast. He thanketh your lordship for the French wine; it is the best that came this year in England.

JOHN HUSEE
in a letter to Lord Lisle, 27 April 1536
The Lisle Letters

A dozen men wearing simple tunics, and trousers rolled up to mid thigh, are standing around in the press . . . their bulging calf muscles stained with wine. At a given signal, the violin gives a trill, and the men dance, their naked feet crushing the grapes they tread on as they turn and turn about. The juice flows, rosy and clouded. It is the wine that you and I will drink in four or five years' time . . . I look at the feet of the dancing men, and I can't help feeling my enthusiasm wane . . . It would be quite a different matter if instead the grapes were tread by seductive dancers, specially selected for their charms, with white plumpish legs and those little feet with pretty pink nails.

LOUIS BERTALL
La Vigne, 1878

. . . barefooted, and ankle-deep in the thick magenta juice, were the treaders of the winepress . . . We had always hoped against hope for *sabots*. The proprietor . . . hastened to explain that the fermenting process purified everything.

E. SOMERVILLE & MARTIN ROSS
In the Vine Country

Of the Red wines of Bordeaux the Lafitte is the
most choice and delicate, and is characterized by
its silky softness on the palate and its charming
perfume, which partakes of the violet and the
raspberry. The Latour has a fuller body, and at
the same time a considerable aroma, but wants
the softness of the Lafitte. The Château
Margaux is, on the other hand, lighter, and
possesses all the delicate qualities of the Lafitte,
except that it has not quite so high a flavour.
The Haut-Brion, again, has more spirit and body
than any of the preceding, but it is rough, when
used, and requires to be kept six or seven years
in the wood; while the others become fit for
bottling in much less time. These are the first-
rate wines of the Bordelais.

ANON
The Wine-Drinker's Manual, 1830

*Of the more than 2,000 châteaux
in the Bordeaux region, 200 of
the best are classified. The
official classification made in
1855 still holds good, with the
top premiers crûs being
Châteaux Lafite, Latour,
Margaux and Haut-Brion. It was only in 1973
that Château Mouton-Rothschild joined this select
band, owing to the untiring efforts of Baron
Philippe de Rothschild over many years.*

*It seems astonishing but Bordeaux alone makes
more wine in a year than Australia.*

Those wonderful vintages from 1864 to 1878 with which Nature tried to console mankind for the coming of the scourge of Phylloxera, the Lafite of 1864, the Margaux of 1871, the Latour of 1875 – they are indeed the swan-song of Bordeaux – have in our days become as precious as that virtuous woman, who the Preacher tells us is above rubies.

CHARLES WALTER BERRY
Viniana

From 'Punch' in 1890

A sale of pre-phylloxera claret took place at Christie's in London in 1967, featuring wines such as 1864 Lafite and 1858 Latour from Lord Rosebery's cellar. An 1865 Lafite in particular was pronounced to be 'superb'. The prices fetched were considered astronomical, but by today's standards 'quite a bargain'.

. . . to the Royall Oak Tavern . . . and here drank a sort of French wine, called Ho Bryan, that hath a good and particular taste that I never met with.

SAMUEL PEPYS
Diary, 10 April 1663

Still extremely tannic and nowhere near maturity. The finish must be experienced to be believed, as it must last ninety seconds or more . . . In terms of aging potential, it may be the wine of the decade.

ROBERT M. PARKER of a 1975 La Mission Haut-Brion, *Bordeaux,* 1986
Mr Parker gives this wine a rating of 100, and suggests that it will mature between 2005 and 2050.

Immensely impressive,. . . but felt like cold pebbles in the mouth . . . Extraordinary medicinal bouquet, TCP and bandages, which happily simmered down. 'Pickled peach' noted earlier, also iodine . . . Mahler with a touch of Bartok.

MICHAEL BROADBENT of the same wine
The Great Vintage Wine Book II, 1991

There is far more interest to be gained from a bottle of claret than there is from a bottle of burgundy . . . I believe that it is the comparatively slow maturity rate of claret that makes it so intriguing to the regular drinker.

ROBIN DON
The Compleat Imbiber, 1971

Many other very good wines known as 'Bourgeois growths' are to be found in the Médoc; and the districts of Graves and St Emilion also produce wines which bear a very high reputation. It does not either at all follow that the better of these 'unclassed' wines are always, as a matter of course, inferior to the 'classed' growths, although technically they may rank after them. With Clarets, as in fact with all wines, the vintage is of far greater importance than the name, however illustrious it may be. A Bourgeois growth of a good year, for instance, is very much to be preferred to a 'classed' growth of a bad one.

C. E. HAWKER
Chats About Wine, 1907

I remember, when dining a few years ago with a friend at an inn in the village of Margaux, within a stone's throw of the Château, we were much amused on finding the wine so very bad that we could drink it only with water.

THOMAS GEORGE SHAW
Wine, the Vine, and the Cellar, 1863

. . . Good claret doesn't exist . . . I certainly didn't find it at Bordeaux, where I drank a most vulgar fluid; and it is of course notorious that a large part of mankind is occupied in vainly looking for it.

HENRY JAMES
A Little Tour in France, 1884

The white Bordeaux wines vary from the thinnest acidulous disembodied wine to the lordly Sauternes. Of the Château Yquem I have spoken elsewhere as a wine of perfection, in which a large quantity of the richness of the grapes becomes blended by age into a body of inexhaustible fragrance.

DR ROBERT DRUITT
Report on Cheap Wines, Their Use in Diet and Medicine, 1873

The vintage in these districts is altogether different from the vintage in any other part of the world; for the grapes are allowed to hang until they are ripe and begin to decay, and then they are collected berry by berry, only such berries being taken as fully answer to the description 'ripe and rotten'. The definition of 'rottenness', however, requires a qualification, which is also well-known on the Rhine, namely, it must be 'sweet'. The decay applies in reality only to the husk, or a portion of it, while the flesh of the grape remains sound underneath it. We have been present at Château Suduiraut on an occasion when the vintagers passed through the vineyard for the tenth time, each time collecting single berries.

J.L.W. THUDICHUM
A Treatise on Wines, 1894

59

Rich Burgundy

I'll sing you a song of Burgundy,
Of the sunny slopes where the grapes are
   grown,
Beloved of the Wine-God, beloved of me,
On the warm Côte d'Or in the country of
   Beaune.
WILLIAM BLISS

I never shall forget the glorious September afternoon, when, standing on the old ramparts of Beaune, the whole range of hills rose before us, each bearing some honoured name; with Pommard and Volnay in front. The next day we drove about twenty miles to the south of Beaune, visiting on our way Volnay, Pommard, Meursault and Montrachet, where I heard the young wine chirping in the casks, like an infant Bacchus in its cradle. We had a long drive through a country *bien accidenté*, passing Chagny and many villages intermixed with vineyards. My friend pointed out the harmony, as it were, of the country – 'the Golden Slope' – the *Côte d'Or*; how the hills produced wine, the plains wheat, whilst cattle graze on the low ground by the river; and the poplars supply a light wood for packing-cases and double casks.

DR ROBERT DRUITT
Report on Cheap Wines, Their Use in Diet and Medicine, 1873

The wines which have given such celebrity to Burgundy, grow only on the Cote, an extent of about five leagues long, and half a league wide. They begin at Chambertin, and go through Vougeau, Romanie, Veaune, Nuys, Beaune, Pommard, Voulenay, Meursault, and end at Monrachet. Those of the two last are white, the others red. Chambertin, Vougeau and Veaune are strongest, and will bear transportation and keeping . . . Voulenay is the best of the other reds, equal in flavor to Chambertin, etc., but being lighter, will not keep . . . It is pretended that the adjoining vineyards produce the same qualities, but that belonging to obscure individuals, they have not obtained a name, and therefore sell as other wines.

THOMAS JEFFERSON
Travel Journals, March 1787

Chambertin lay in the direction of Vougeot, but by a very bad road. The land under vines is in general very much subdivided throughout France, but here the properties are off less extent than anywhere I have been. Five or six proprietors often divide among them a piece of ground not exceeding an acre in extent . . . The vigneron said that the wine produced to the left of the by-road we were travelling was inferior to that on the right, which was higher and drier.

JAMES BUSBY
Journal of a Tour through Some of the Vineyards of Spain and France, 1834

The King: Chambertin
The Queen: Romanée-Conti
The Regent: Clos-Vougeot
Princes of the Blood: Romanée, Musigny, Nuits,
    Bonnes-Mares
First Cousin of Chambertin: Richebourg
Standard-bearer: Corton
Dukes and Duchesses: Hospices de Beaune,
    Volnay, Pommard, Beaune, Savigny, Santenay,
    Mercurey, Montrachet, Meursault, Chablis
        family tree of Burgundy wines
        quoted by E. de CLERMONT-TONNERRE
        Almanach des bonnes choses de France

This classification is only valid in the absolute.
The reality is that in some years, for climatic
reasons, Chambertin is surpassed by Nuits-
Saint-Georges, Richebourg or Clos-Vougeot . . .
There is constant rivalry between these wines,
and sometimes the primacy in a particular year
will fall to an outsider flavoured by the sun . . .
Rather than a monarchy with a rigid hierarchy,
the wines of Burgundy form an aristocratic
republic where each succeeds according to merit.
    MAURICE DES OMBIAUX
    Le Gotha des vins de France, 1925

62

'You have not told me yet the vintage or growth of this Burgundy . . . Is it Côte de Nuits or Côte de Beaune? Well, I should unhesitatingly say the former, there always seems to be more 'grandeur' in the wines of the Côte de Nuits, and . . . I should venture an opinion that this wine emanates from Bertin's field, known all the world over as Cham(p)bertin . . .

Now for the vintage. . . It certainly is very old and very well-preserved. Anything older than 1864 I cannot remember: it hardly resembles the sixty-fours I have in mind, but they were Richebourg, a little hard, whereas this is not. 1865, yes, I have drunk some excellent 1865, but it was some years ago, and I do not think that they would be so well preserved as this – no, not 1865 . . . I tell you – yes – I believe it is 1869; what a gem of a wine, and so is this; am I right? . . .'

'Wrong! 1865 Chambertin!'

> CHARLES WALTER BERRY
> *A Miscellany of Wine*, 1932

It may be blasphemous to call it 'coarse', but it seems to me that it 'doth something grow to' coarseness . . . It was Napoleon's favourite, and the fact rather 'speaks' its qualities, good and not so good.

> GEORGE SAINTSBURY of Chambertin
> *Notes on a Cellar-Book*, 1920

The Clos-Vougeôt is a large vineyard surrounded by a wall, and is so celebrated, that when a French regiment marches past, it halts and presents arms.

THOMAS GEORGE SHAW
Wine, the Vine, and the Cellar, 1863

The four old presses in the press-room are marvels of solidity, and are, I believe, 300 years old. The greatest care is taken that the grapes shall be crushed, and that the contents of the *cuve* or fermenting vat shall be equally mixed; a care that is laudable, though the means employed are not so; because for this purpose men go naked into the vats, to stir up and mix all the grape skins and husks, and, it is said, to promote fermentation by the warmth of their bodies.

DR ROBERT DRUITT at Clos de Vougeot
Report on Cheap Wines, Their Use in Diet and Medicine, 1873

Clos de Vougeot is described in a modern wine guide as an unreliable 'grand cru', but as 'wonderfully fleshy' when good.

Burgundy I always think of as the woman of thirty: it has more body than claret, is richer, more generous, with a finer perfume; but it is very intoxicating and should be used with self restraint.

FRANK HARRIS
My Life and Loves

Beaujolais is little known, as a *cru* and a region, both by gastronomes and by tourists. As a *cru,* it is sometimes taken to be simply a tail of Burgundy . . . There is a tendency to think that Morgon is but a pale imitation of Corton [a Burgundy wine]. This unforgivable and gross mistake is made by people who drink without discrimination . . . The wine of Beaujolais has its own special qualities, a bouquet which is unmistakable.

GABRIEL CHEVALLIER
Clochemerle

All the best Beaujolais wines are produced in the northern part of the region, and among the names to qualify for the Beaujolais-Villages appellation are Juliénas, Fleurie, Moulin-à-Vent, Morgon, Brouilly and Côtes de Brouilly.

All common cheap French red wines seem now to have got the name of Beaujolais as white have that of Chablis.

THOMAS GEORGE SHAW
Wine, the Vine, and the Cellar, 1863

What bard today
Can live like old Khayyám? It's not the same –
A loaf and Thou and Tesco's Beaujolais.

WENDY COPE
Making Cocoa for Kingsley Amis, 1986

A French Primer

Dr Robert Druitt, in his book 'Report on Cheap Wines', referred to 'the large and exquisite set of phrases which the French have devised for the description of the qualities of wine'. Here are a few of them, together with some modern terms.

Cru: the vineyard or estate

cru classé: classed growth

tête de cuvée: from the best cask in a grower's cellar

en cave: in the cellar

mise en bouteilles: a term often queried by those with a penchant for French wine and for grammar, as to why the feminine is used when *vin* is masculine. The answer is that *mise* is here not the past participle but the noun – 'bottling', not 'bottled at'.

tonneaux: barrels

goût de terroir: a very French notion that the soil, aspect, climate and indigenous plants give the grape and therefore the wine a special taste.

vin biologique: organic wine

macération carbonique: a vinification method in
which whole grapes are fermented, for wines to
be drunk quickly, such as *beaujolais nouveau.*

vin de primeur: young, new wine

vin de garde: good for keeping

pourriture noble: the 'noble rot' *botrytis cineraria,*
which is essential for the production of
Sauternes and other dessert wines.

crémant: term for upmarket sparkling wine

raisins: grapes, not raisins

chambrer: to bring to room temperature

frapper: to chill

corsé: full-bodied

flasque, mou: flabby, insipid

moelleux: neither dry nor sweet. Also *doux,
naturel*

âpreté: excess of tannin

velouté: velvety quality

qui sent le bouchon: corked

être entre deux vins: to be tipsy

The French regard wine as a national possession
all their very own, just like their 360 varieties of
cheese and their culture.

ROLAND BARTHES
Mythologies

Wine is the blood of France.

LOUIS BERTALL
La Vigne, 1878

The Loire

There is one only course to pursue if you wish to taste the best wines of France . . . It is to ask the proprietor of any restaurant in which you may eat, what wines he suggests should go with the dishes you have ordered.

FORD MADOX FORD
Provence

At the little inn at Chenonceaux the *cuisine* was not only excellent, but the service was graceful. We were waited on by mademoiselle and her mamma; it was so that mademoiselle alluded to the elder lady, as she uncorked for us a bottle of Vouvray mousseux. We were very comfortable, very genial; we even went so far as to say to each other that Vouvray mousseux was a delightful wine.

HENRY JAMES
A Little Tour in France, 1884

Vouvray, two leagues from Tours; wines of good quality, sweet and *liquoreux* the first year; by age they become *spiritueux,* then *moelleux,* with a very pleasant flavour, and very *capiteux*.

ANDRÉ JULLIEN
The Topography of All the Known Vineyards, 1824

The wines of Bourgueil have a subtle and fine raspberry perfume, and their bouquet and other qualities make them both like bordeaux and burgundy. The Chinon wines are less strong, but have an even more pronounced scent of raspberry.

MAURICE DES OMBIAUX
Le Gotha des vins de France, 1925

Robust Rhônes

The valley of the Rhone is indescribable. I have never yet known what sunlight is; I have never seen autumn colours on trees . . . And the vineyards, two hundred miles of them. The dead vine leaves are sometimes patches of brilliant scarlet. But how am I to describe the sunlight – the atmosphere – the distances?

GEORGE GISSING
in a letter to his sister Ellen, 28 October 1888

The red wines of Châteauneuf-du-Pape possess remarkable tonic properties. They diffuse a heat within and ensure a lasting glow which is a gift entirely their own and one which is not due to any greater alcoholic strength than other red wines.

ANDRÉ SIMON
A Wine Primer

As to the flavour one might easily go into dythyrambs. Wine-slang talks of the 'finish' in such cases, but this was so full and so complicated that it never seemed to come to a finish. You could meditate on it, and it kept up with your meditations.

> GEORGE SAINTSBURY writing about a red Hermitage of 1846 (drunk 40 years later), *Notes on a Cellar-Book*, 1920

White Hermitage is a still more precious wine, between the dry and sweet wines in taste. It will keep to a considerable age, some say to a hundred years. It is considered the finest white wine of France; it takes an amber colour by age, and should be kept from the air to the last moment before drinking. As only about a hundred and twenty pieces are made annually, it is necessary to be particular in securing the real growth.

> CYRUS REDDING
> *Every Man His Own Butler*, 1839

It is two thousand five hundred years since the Greeks and Romans introduced the vine to Provence, so it seems surprising not to find there the best vineyards and the best cultivation: it is neither lack of sun nor any deficiency of the soil, but the lack of care of the inhabitants.

> ALEXANDRE DUMAS
> *Le Grand Dictionnaire de cuisine*, 1873

There are little local vineyards producing wines just as good as all but the great classic vineyards in their best years. For myself I drink with perfect contentment year in year out a little domain wine grown not far away from where I live, it costing me, when I have bottled it, Frs 42 for a barrique of 25 bottles – or less than two francs the bottle.

FORD MADOX FORD
Provence

I was no more than three when my father . . . gave me a full liqueur glass of a reddish-brown wine sent to him from his native Southern France; the Muscat Wine of Frontignan. It was like a sun-stroke, or love at first sight.

COLETTE
Prisons et paradis

•

To make Muscat wines, the grapes (as with other white wines) are left till quite ripe, and the stalks of the bunches are twisted on the vine, till they become withered and dried in the sun; the grapes are afterwards gathered, pressed, and the *must* is left to ferment; but as this juice is glutinous and syrupy, the sun having deprived it of a great part of its water, the operation takes place imperfectly. Muscat wine can thus only be made in warm countries, as in Languedoc and Provence, where the sun has great force. The best wines are from Frontignan and Lunel.

ANON
The Wine-Drinker's Manual, 1830

71

Rhineland

Ring for your valet – bid him quickly bring
Some hock and soda-water, then you'll know
A pleasure worthy Xerxes, the great king.
For not blest sherbet, sublimed with snow,
Nor the first sparkle of the desert spring,
Nor Burgundy in all its sun-set glow,
After long travel, ennui, love, or slaughter,
Vie with that draught of hock and soda-water.

LORD BYRON
Don Juan

It is to be regretted that there are so few good
vintages on the Rhine. Extraordinarily fine as its
wine is in good years, it is proportionately bad in
others; it is then unpleasant, and its consumption
is almost confined to the country itself . . . A few
proprietors are in the habit, in bad years, of
mixing sugar with their wine, to make it more
agreeable.

THOMAS GEORGE SHAW
Wine, the Vine, and the Cellar, 1863

The most renowned growths are found in a
district called the Rheingau, which is a most
prolific stretch of vineyards extending for about
ten miles on the right bank of the Rhine between
Mayence and Rüdesheim. It is said that the vine
was first cultivated in these parts as early as the
third century, and was subsequently very greatly
extended by mediaeval monks, particularly those

of the monasteries of Johannisberg and Eberback. The principal vineyards lie between the Taunus mountains in the north and the Rhine in the south.

C.E. HAWKER
Chats About Wine, 1907

The finest possible wine, illustrative of what nature, aided by industry and improved by science, can effect . . . Johannesberger, the Château-Margaux of the Rhine . . .

EDWARD L. BECKWITH
Practical Notes on Wine, 1868

I may say that the man who is not satisfied with a good Rüdesheimer or Hochheimer at 50s to 70s must be very hard to please. These are the wines drunk by Pallas Athene at the council feasts of the gods. The variety and complex harmony of their body and flavour can only be compared to a chord held down on some full organ.

DR ROBERT DRUITT
Report on Cheap Wines, Their Use in Diet and Medicine, 1873

By its methods and results Hochheim is really a part, and a very typical one, of the Rheingau. The Riesling grape here attains its highest development; it is, when perfect, light brown and transparent, not green. The stalk of the perfectly ripe bunch must be dry and shrivelled, like that of raisins.

J.L.W. THUDICHUM
A Treatise on Wines, 1894

The most fatal scourges to the wine grower in the northern parts of Europe are frosts in April and May . . . To obviate this they have recourse to artificial means, as, an hour before sunrise burning litter among the vines, particularly on the Rhine. Four persons are sufficient to smoke an arpent of vines, which they effect by torches of straw. They continue to operate until the sun shines on the plants. The melted frost falls off. It would seem, therefore, that the injury arose from the sun's action on the frost.

CYRUS REDDING
A History and Description of Modern Wines,
1833

Rhein wein, fein wein,
Necker wein, lecre wein,
Franken wein, tranken wein,
Mosel wein, unnosel wein.
GERMAN SAYING

Chianti Land

In proportion as nature has been more bountiful here than in other countries, have the culture of the plant and the manufacture of the wine, been neglected by the indolence of the people. The vines are left to luxuriate amidst fences, or the boundaries of fields, and this rude growth supplies the Italian peasant with sufficient wine for his own consumption.

ANON
The Wine-Drinker's Manual, 1830

Viewing the geographical position of Italy, and knowing that it is mountainous and hilly from north to south, it is surprising it has never yet acquired the reputation of producing any good wine . . . Throughout the whole country vines are grown, and wine made; and I do not believe that better qualities could be produced in any part of Europe; but it must never be forgotten that there is no plant which requires such incessant care as the vine, and no operation demanding more skill, experience, and patience than making wine. The exercise of patience requires the combination of capital, and capital seeks a compensating benefit.

In countries where wine is so abundant that all may drink it, little money value is attached to it, and it is consequently neglected; a remark which applies to every wine-land, where there is not an external demand.

THOMAS GEORGE SHAW
Wine, the Vine, and the Cellar, 1863

In particular districts of Italy, however, it is by no means rare to meet with good wine, and as in many instances both care and industry are exercised in its management, the ancient fame of its vinous produce may yet emerge from the common darkness that for ages has enshrouded the land; for shall it be forgotten whence came the nectar of which Anacreon used to sing? or where grew the grapes for the vintages so lovingly painted in Virgil? If Italy could produce superlative wines in the times of Augustus, why not now, with an undiminished sun and unimpaired soil, and every modern appliance to boot?

JAMES L. DENMAN
The Vine and Its Fruit, 1864

Tuscany is one huge vineyard and olive-ground. What would be fields and common hedges in England, are here a mass of orchards, producing wine and oil, so that the sight becomes tiresome in its very beauty. About noon, all the labourers, peasantry, and small shop-keepers in Tuscany, may be imagined taking their flask of wine. You see them all about Florence fetching it under their arms.

LEIGH HUNT
in the notes for his translation of *Bacco in Toscana* by Francesco Redi

Italy with all her natural advantages has not yet learnt how to produce a really fine dry wine. Apart from a limited number of special growths, such as the Barolo of Piedmont, the Chianti of Tuscany, the Orvieto and Vino dell' Est of the Roman States, the Lacryma Christi of Naples, and the Zucco of Cosenza, almost all her wines lack flavour and bouquet. They are invariably rich in colour, and those of the South are remarkably alcoholic, but these qualities . . . fail to atone for the want of agreeable taste and aroma. It is but just to add, however, that of late years considerable progress has been made in the right direction . . . The principal cause of the mediocrity of the Italian wines arises from their imperfect fermentation, which renders them liable to become muddy or turn into aceteous acid.

HENRY VIZETELLY
The Wines of the World, 1875

Another notable wine is Lacrima Cristi, which probably, like the Liebfraumilch of the Rhineland, owes part of its vogue to its curious name.

C.E. HAWKER
Chats About Wine, 1907

. . . some sparkling Lacrima Cristi, which suggested ginger beer alternately stirred up with a stick of chocolate and a large sulphur match.

GEORGE SAINTSBURY
Notes on a Cellar-Book, 1920

Amarone . . . a wine of incredible depth, bouquet and breed. Forget about that, however, and listen to the name – preferably pronounced by Luciano Pavarotti –Am-mahr-roh-nay; a siren song, a seduction.

LEONARD BERNSTEIN
The Official Guide to Wine Snobbery

Italy vies with France as the world's largest producer, making one fifth of the total, and is the largest exporter. The Denominazione d'Origine Controllata was introduced in 1963, and a further 'e Garantita' has been added for wines such as Barolo, Barbaresco, Vino Nobile di Montepulciano and Brunello di Montalcino. Native grape varities include nebbiolo, sangiovese, barbera, lambrusco and verdicchio.

We have only begun to do what the French did long ago, to co-ordinate our wine varieties with their ideal habitat. It seems hard to believe that after six hundred years we still have so much to accomplish. In a sense, Italy is a young wine country with so much potential.

PIERO ANTINORI
head of the wine producers Marchesi Antinori of Florence (established in 1385), quoted in *Christie's Wine Companion*, 1987

The Rest of Europe

It was vintage time in the valleys on the Swiss side of the Pass of the Great Saint Bernard, and along the banks of the Lake of Geneva. The air there was charged with the scent of gathered grapes. Baskets, troughs, and tubs of grapes, stood in the dim village door-ways, stopped the steep and narrow village streets, and had been carrying all day along the roads and lanes. Grapes, split and crushed under foot, lay about everywhere . . . A pity that no ripe touch of this generous abundance could be given to the thin, hard, stony wine, which after all was made from the grapes!

CHARLES DICKENS
Little Dorrit

As a rule, the Swiss, as wine-growers, must be admired more for the industry and perseverance they have shown than for any great result they have attained.

EDWARD L. BECKWITH
Practical Notes on Wine, 1868

Spain is a grand country for drinking . . . because the Spaniards to not approach the matter too reverentially . . . you would never catch the French calling one of their finest clarets 'Uncle Bill', which is after all, the rough equivalent of *Tio Pepe*.

QUENTIN CREWE
International Pocket Food Book

80

Already in ancient times the Greeks would have added pine-cones to their amphoras of wine, under the pretext that this tree had provided the thyrsus of Bacchus. Modern Greeks have unfortunately maintained this habit, which makes their wines impossible to drink for anybody else than the Greeks themselves.

> ALEXANDRE DUMAS
> *Le Grand Dictionnaire de cuisine*, 1873

Our forefathers knew Hungarian wine very well, although their name has since been blotted out for a time by port, war, and prejudice. Sir Edward Barry quotes . . . that 'the Buda wine is very like Burgundy, and perhaps equal to it . . . A great quantity used to be sent to England in the reign of James the First overland by Breslau and Hamburgh, and it was the favourite wine of the court, and all over the kingdom.'

> DR ROBERT DRUITT
> *Report on Cheap Wines, Their Use in Diet and Medicine*, 1873

The exposure, the climate, the mode of cultivation of the vine, and the mode of making the wine will of course influence the lightness, richness, taste, and bouquet of the ultimate product; but the Pineau, wherever grown, will reproduce the main qualities of the Burgundy wine, and the Carbenet [sic], wherever grown will recall that of the Médoc.

> J.L.W. THUDICHUM
> *A Treatise on Wines*, 1894

Sunny Australia

On comparison of the various figures it will be found that the colonies of South Australia and Victoria far outstrip the older colony of New South Wales, the colony of South Australia standing first and foremost as the fosterer of the vine and wine-making.

HENRY VIZETELLY
The Wines of the World, 1875

It was German Lutherans, escaping from religious persecution, who started the Barossa Valley vineyards in South Australia in 1842, six years after the colony had been founded. Barossa Valley is the headquarters of Penfolds and Orlando, and while its vineyards amount to only ten percent of the total, it produces sixty per cent of Australian wine, processing grapes from other areas.

Now we have every reason to believe that in South Australia we can produce wines in all respects equal, and in some respects superior, to those of France. Let our first-class vignerons have faith in the wines they make pure and simple, and carefully eschew all tampering with them, and doctoring them, and let them sell them at as moderate a price as they can afford until the taste for them is firmly established, when they will become a necessity, and then we have no doubt they will be able to command highly remunerative prices. It is as certain as anything can be that the manufacture of wine will become one of the chief articles of South Australian produce.

THOMAS GEORGE SHAW
Wine, the Vine, and the Cellar, 1863

It does not seem likely that Australian vintners will ever endeavour to enter into effective rivalry with the vignerons of Europe, but in the event of their desiring Englishmen to take the wines of the Antipodes seriously, Australians must conform to French and German practice as regards the classification of their produce. At present, by far the greater part of the annual output is mixed together and shipped under the name of 'Australian Burgundy', with no description beyond the shipper's name or brand . . . The connoisseur must not be expected to show much interest in the matter until he is in a position to compare the vineyard or region with another, and also to contrast different years.

C.E. HAWKER
Chats About Wine, 1907

. . . and California

Very good in its way
Is the Verzenay
Or the Sillery soft and creamy,
But Catawba wine
Has a taste more divine,
More dulcet, delicious, and dreamy.
>   H.W. LONGFELLOW
>   'Catawba Wine'

The most important vineyards are those of Ohio, Missouri, and Indiana. Wine is also made in Western Virginia, the State of New York, Pensylvania, and Maryland. But the most celebrated is in Cincinnati, where there are large vineyards . . . who have gained a high reputation for their sparkling Catawba . . . California seems better adapted for producing good wine . . . One firm is stated to have produced, in 1858, . . . in all 23,000 gallons.
>   THOMAS GEORGE SHAW
>   *Wine, the Vine, and the Cellar*, 1863

The soil in the wine-growing districts of California is said to resemble closely that of some of the notable vineyards in France, and as climate and soil are very important factors in wine production – nationality not counting for much in the final result – it is not surprising that these wines find a certain amount of favour.
>   C.E. HAWKER
>   *Chats About Wine*, 1907

California producers have finally accepted that they have a Mediterranean climate, and are acting accordingly.

ANTHONY DIAS BLUE
quoted in *Decanter* Magazine, October 1995

The vines of Peru afford delicious grapes of various kinds in the vicinity of Lima, but, from the great demand for table use, little or no wine is made near that city. Those of Chile produce better fruit for wine than Peru, yet as the consumption is small, the vine-grounds in that province are much neglected. The red grape is the most cultivated, and is remarkable for richness and fragrance, the muscatel far exceeding that of Spain, as well in the fruit as the wine it yields. The vines are trained *en espalier*. Nothing can equal the beauty of some of the clusters of the Chilean grape.

JAMES L. DENMAN
The Vine and Its Fruit, 1864

Chile has been extremely successful in exporting to Britain and the United States in the last decade. But the largest wine producing country around is in fact Argentina which comes in as the sixth largest in the world, making three times as much wine as Australia. So far it has exported little because its production methods are old fashioned and it caters for home demand.

Old Sherry

I wonder if you have ever heard of the old Bishop of Seville. He lived to a great age (over 100 years) and always seemed to be hale and hearty . . .

'There is only one reason,' he said: 'Every day since I can remember I have consumed one bottle of good Sherry wine, except when I have not felt well, and then I have consumed two.'

CHARLES WALTER BERRY
A Miscellany of Wine, 1932

The citizens of Bristol call sherry 'Bristol milk' through the happy custom of moistening the lips of their newborn babies with the sweet, rich, olorosos which older babes may still purchase under the name Bristol Milk.

WALTER JAMES
Antipasto, 1957

When Madeira is originally fine, and kept till quite ripe, there is a soft fullness, with a delicious, pungent, delicate high flavour that surpasses every other kind, and compared to which even the best sherry is tasteless and flavourless.

THOMAS GEORGE SHAW
Wine, the Vine, and the Cellar, 1863

I know no wine of its class that can beat Madeira when at its best . . . Certainly a real old Bual or Sercial of the times before 1850 – I have drunk 1780 Madeira when it was nearly ninety years old and in perfection – was a thing to say grace for and remember. In fact, I think Madeira and Burgundy carry combined intensity and complexity of vinous delights further than any other wines.

GEORGE SAINTSBURY
Notes on a Cellar-Book, 1920

In Tokay there is a bouquet that is as subtle to the tongue as Oloroso Sherry and when you have quaffed it the fragrance seems to possess overtones that resound like a note echoing on the piano-strings through all their harmonies.

WALTER STARKIE
Raggle-Taggle

It never was a wine: only a prince of liqueurs.

GEORGE SAINTSBURY of Tokay
Notes on a Cellar-Book, 1920

Magisterial Port

He then rang the bell, and having ordered two fresh glasses to be brought, he went out and presently returned with a small pint bottle, which he uncorked with his own hand; then sitting down he said, 'The wine that I bring here is port of eighteen hundred and eleven, the year of the comet, the best vintage on record; the wine which we have been drinking,' he added, 'is good, but not to be compared with this, which I never sell, and which I am chary of. When you have drunk some of it, I think you will own that I have conferred an obligation upon you'. He then filled the glasses, the wine which he poured out diffusing an aroma through the room.

> GEORGE BORROW
> *The Romany Rye*

To-night Fanny, Dora and I dined at Langley House. Mr Ashe was particularly agreeable. He gave me a bottle of superb 1847 port which we finished together.

> REVD FRANCIS KILVERT
> *Diary*, 30 December 1871

Never have a small glass of port, my lad. It just goes wambling around looking for damage to do. Have a large glass. It settles down and does you good.

> attributed to LORD GODDARD

Host: *'Let me give you some of this port. It is the
very last bottle of my '47.'*

Guest: *'Well, just a very little. I don't really like it
but the fact is I've been suffering from cold
feet.'*

from *Punch* in 1907

He drank it as port should be drunk – a trial of the bouquet; a slow sip; a rather larger and slightly less slow one, and so on; but never a gulp; and during the drinking his face exchanged its usual bluff and almost brusque aspect for the peculiar blandness . . . which good wine gives to worthy countenances.

GEORGE SAINTSBURY
Notes on a Cellar-Book, 1920

Having slowly ingurgitated and meditated upon this precious draught, and turned its flavour over and over with an aspect of potent Judicial wisdom (one might have thought that he was weighing mankind in the balance), the old lawyer heaved, and said, sharpening his lips over the admirable vintage, 'The world is in a very sad state, I fear, Sir Austin!'

His client gazed at him queerly.

'But that,' Mr Thompson added immediately, ill-concealing by his gaze the glowing intestinal congratulations going on within him, 'that is, I think you would say, Sir Austin, if I could but prevail upon you – a tolerably good character wine!' . . .

The old lawyer sat down to finish his glass, saying, that such a wine was not to be had everywhere.

GEORGE MEREDITH
The Ordeal of Richard Feverel

Brandies of Wondrous Age

. . . brandies of wondrous age, most of which were already in the cellars when the battle of Waterloo was fought.

> LT. COL. NATHANIEL NEWNHAM-DAVIS
> writing about the cellars of the Café Anglais
> *The Gourmet's Guide to Europe*, 1908

After a meal a small glass of brandy is, to my mind, not so much a luxury as a necessity; it is a wonderful aid to digestion, and if old and fine, oh! so delectable!

> CHARLES WALTER BERRY
> *A Miscellany of Wine*, 1932

After dinner, the cognac bottle is produced and the pastor fills his tumbler half full of spirit, and but lightly dashes it with water. It is cognac and not brandy, for your chapel minister thinks it an affront if anything more common than the best French liquor is put before him; he likes it strong, and with it his long clay pipe. Very frequently another minister, sometimes two or three, come in at the same time, and take the same dinner and afterwards form a genial circle with cognac

91

and tobacco, when the room speedily becomes full
of smoke and the bottle of brandy   soon
disappears.

RICHARD JEFFERIES
Field and Hedgerow

I once unintentionally deceived one of the really
great connoisseurs. . . . I had had some really
wonderful 1895 Apple Jack that came from a
Princely cellar . . . The Calvados was in
magnums with the princely seal very large on the
bottles but the date written only on a paper label.
So, that distillation being famous, I had a
number of friends and my little lot had lasted
only a year or so . . . But at the same time as I
had bought that lot I had bought a quantity of
1920 from the same cellar. It was a very good
fluid but *not* 1895 . . .

My friend the connoisseur had come however
so long after the 1895 had been exhausted that
what I gave him, without after thought, was the
1920 – from an exactly identical magnum, with
the same princely seal and the paper with the
date naturally gone.

My friend smelt it, tasted it; threw back his
head, breathed out through his nose. and then
said reverentially: 'Ah, nothing will ever beat
your 1895.'

FORD MADOX FORD
Provence

Frothy Champagne

Mr Crotchet: Champagne, doctor?
The Rev. Dr. Folliott: Most willingly. But you will permit my drinking it while it sparkles. I hold it a heresy to let it deaden in my hand.

> THOMAS LOVE PEACOCK
> *Crotchet Castle*

It is a mistake to suppose that Champagne is spoiled if not drunk the day that it is opened. By corking it again, tying the cork firmly down, then turning the bottle mouth downwards, it will be found good for a long time.

> THOMAS GEORGE SHAW
> *Wine, the Vine, and the Cellar*, 1863

Even champagne, after it has been so long in ice as to become very cold, is not to be compared to the same wine when brought out of a cold cellar. The flavour gets *locked up*, and it is difficult, when in that chilled state, to distinguish the finest from a common quality.

> THOMAS GEORGE SHAW
> *Wine, the Vine, and the Cellar*, 1863

Champagne . . . the sign of a ceremonial dinner. Pretend to despise it, saying: 'It's really not a wine.' Arouses the enthusiasm of petty folk. Russia drinks more of it than France. Has been the medium for spreading French ideas throughout Europe.

GUSTAVE FLAUBERT
Dictionnaire des idées reçues

We prepared ourselves to mark the coming of the New Year with unaccustomed solemnity . . . The reason was that we had set by two bottles of champagne, the real thing, labelled Veuve Clicquot.

ANTON CHEKHOV
Le Recul d'un Chemineau, 1890

As for the French, it is with the extremest rarity that, save at Carnival time, or at a *repas de noces*, they ever touch champagne, which is often alluded to contemptuously, as *'le vin des cocottes'* . . . They are content to make it in order to sell it to the foreigner.

GEORGE AUGUSTUS SALA
Paris Herself Again in 1878-9

The best Champagne comes from the neighbourhood of Rheims and Epernay, but it is more generally known by the name of the shipper than by that of any special locality, and this being the case the prestige of the maker is of course all important. Such names as Cliquot, Heidsieck, Krug, Lanson, Moët, Mumm, Pommery,

Roederer, etc, will occur to everyone as carrying with them a guarantee of high-class quality and excellence.

The most esteemed wines are not the product of any one vineyard, but a blend of many, and it is in this blending, which forms what is called the *cuvée*, that the talent of the real artist is shown.

C.E. HAWKER
Chats About Wine, 1907

To give champagne fair play it ought to be produced at the very beginning of dinner or at any rate after one glass of sherry or Madeira. Any other wines rather unfit the palate for it.

THOMAS WALKER
The Art of Dining, 1881

. . . a banquet at the Imperial Palace . . . with the best of dry Champagne served last of all and not spoilt, as it is invariably in the English-speaking world, by appearing at the beginning.

LAURENS VAN DER POST
First Catch Your Eland

Even for those who dislike Champagne . . . there are two Champagnes one can't refuse: Dom Perignon and the even more superior Cristal . . a chilled fire of such prickly dryness that, swallowed, seems not to have been swallowed at all . . .

TRUMAN CAPOTE
Answered Prayers

. . . one of the elegant extras of life
CHARLES DICKENS

I drink it when I am happy, and when I am sad.
I drink it when I am alone, and I find it
indispensable for any social gathering . . .
Otherwise I never touch it, except when I am
thirsty.
LILIANE BOLLINGER
quoted in a radio interview